Tinker
the Mail Truck

ISBN 979-8-88540-142-5 (paperback)
ISBN 979-8-88540-143-2 (digital)

Christian Faith Publishing
832 Park Avenue
Meadville, PA 16335
www.christianfaithpublishing.com

Printed in the United States of America

Tinker
the Mail Truck

WILLETTE NIVENS

Hello, my name is Tinker, and I'm a mail truck. I'm responsible for getting the mail and my driver around the rural area daily. My driver does a full safety inspection on me each day before we get started.

Once the inspection is done and the mail is ready, she loads me up for our deliveries.

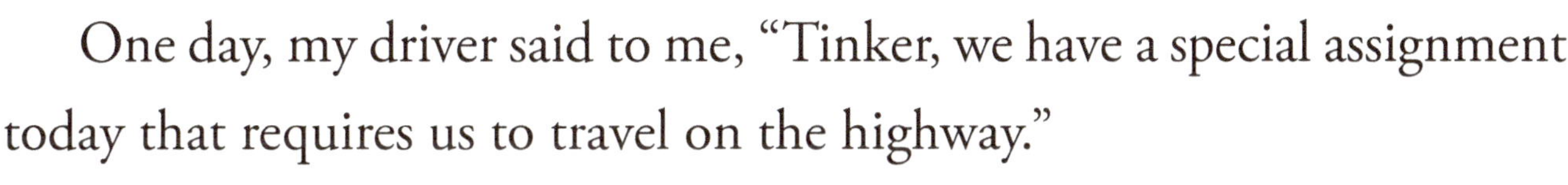

One day, my driver said to me, "Tinker, we have a special assignment today that requires us to travel on the highway."

I told my driver, "I've never been on the highway before, and I'm afraid they have large trucks and cars that are moving really fast, and I don't know if I can keep up."

My driver said to me, "Tinker, you'll be fine. I'm going to drive in the slow lane with the flasher on. You're also passed your morning inspection, which means you can do this."

I was still scared.

She said, "You can do this, Tinker. Just wait and see."

I still wasn't sure because I wasn't used to fast speed.

My driver said to me, "Get ready, Tinker. We are merging onto the highway."

I wasn't excited to be on the highway. My driver cut on my flasher, and we traveled in the slow lane. Then a large truck passed by me, and it shook me from the passing wind. Then more cars and trucks were passing, and I was still shaking. There was no stoplight on the highway, which is what I'm used to. I was so afraid. Then my driver cut off my flasher and used my signal to turn to the right-hand lane.

I asked my driver if we were there yet, and she replied, "Not yet, Tinker, but we are finished with the highway for now."

We are starting our new deliveries, and the speed was slower. We finally finished our deliveries in that neighborhood.

My driver said, "It's time to get back on the highway, Tinker. Are you still afraid?"

I replied, "Yes."

She replied, "There's nothing to be afraid of. Here we go, Tinker.

With my flasher on and us traveling in the slow lane, I became overexcited, and the fear left. I knew what to expect when the big trucks and the fast cars passed by. I shook, but I wasn't afraid because I knew I belong on the highway moving fast.

Once we arrived back at the station, my driver said, "Great job, Tinker."

So until next time, remember you can do anything if you just try.

The end!